Reading
LOG

THIS BOOK BELONGS TO

_____

_____

Index

NO.	BOOK TITLE	GENRE
1		
2		
3		
4		
5		
6		
7		
8		
9		
10		
11		
12		
13		
14		
15		
16		
17		
18		
19		
20		
21		
22		
23		
24		
25		

Index

NO.	BOOK TITLE	GENRE
26		
27		
28		
29		
30		
31		
32		
33		
34		
35		
36		
37		
38		
39		
40		
41		
42		
43		
44		
45		
46		
47		
48		
49		
50		

Index

NO.	BOOK TITLE	GENRE
51		
52		
53		
54		
55		
56		
57		
58		
59		
60		
61		
62		
63		
64		
65		
66		
67		
68		
69		
70		
71		
72		
73		
74		
75		

Index

NO.	BOOK TITLE	GENRE
76		
77		
78		
79		
80		
81		
82		
83		
84		
85		
86		
87		
88		
89		
90		
91		
92		
93		
94		
95		
96		
97		
98		
99		
100		

READING
helps your mind

BLOOM

Books to Read

Book Recommendations

TITLE	AUTHOR	RECOMMENDED BY

Books to Read

Book Recommendations

TITLE	AUTHOR	RECOMMENDED BY

Favorite Quotes

BOOK TITLE	PAGE	QUOTES

Favorite Quotes

BOOK TITLE	PAGE	QUOTES

Books Lent Out

BOOK TITLE	TO WHOM	RETURNED

Books Borrowed

BOOK TITLE	AUTHOR	DATE BORROWED	DATE RETURNED

Anticipated Release

BOOK TITLE	AUTHOR	RELEASE DATE

Bookshelf

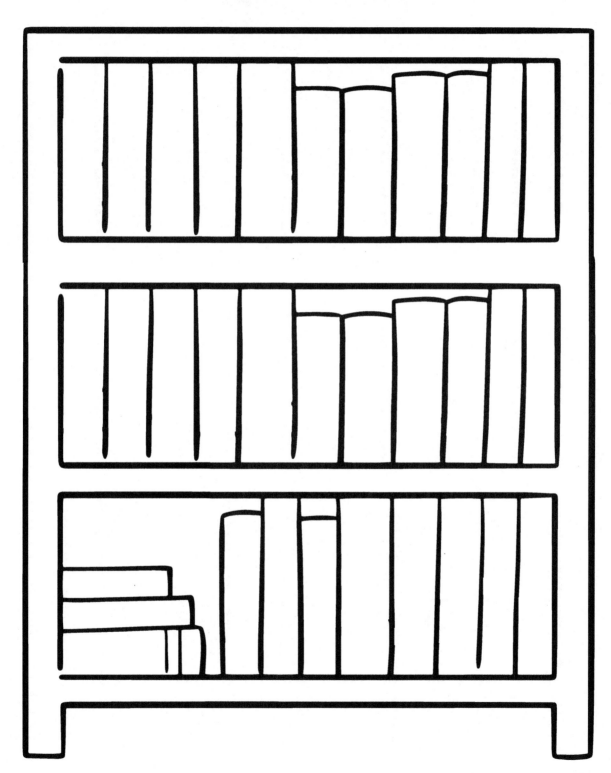

Bookshelf

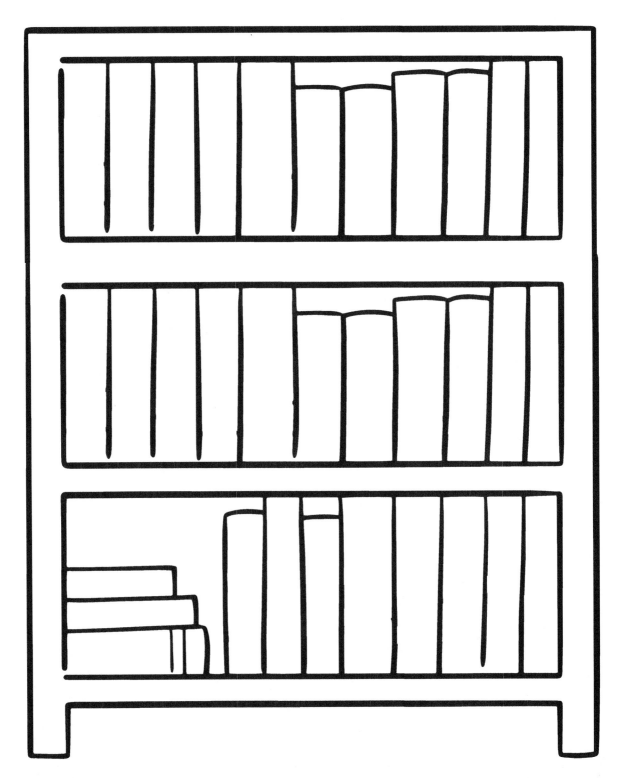

1

BOOK TITLE :

AUTHOR :   **PAGES :**

PUBLISHER :   **PUB DATE :**

○ PAPERBACK   ○ HARDBACK   ○ E-BOOK   ○ AUDIOBOOK   ○ FICTION ○ NON-FICTION

SOURCE : ○ BOUGHT   ○ LOANED   FROM :

Genre :

Start Date :   *Finished Date* :

MY THOUGHTS :   *Rating :* ☆ ☆ ☆ ☆ ☆   *Ease of Reading :* ① ② ③ ④ ⑤

FAVORITE QUOTE : "

WHO WILL I RECOMMEND IT TO?

WHY I READ IT?

WHAT IT INSPIRED ME TO?
(read/learn/visit)

"

2

BOOK TITLE :

AUTHOR :   **PAGES :**

PUBLISHER :   **PUB DATE :**

○ PAPERBACK   ○ HARDBACK   ○ E-BOOK   ○ AUDIOBOOK   ○ FICTION   ○ NON-FICTION

SOURCE :   ○ BOUGHT   ○ LOANED   **FROM :**

Genre :

Start Date :   *Finished Date :*

MY THOUGHTS :   *Rating :* ☆ ☆ ☆ ☆ ☆   *Ease of Reading :* ① ② ③ ④ ⑤

WHO WILL I RECOMMEND IT TO?

WHY I READ IT?

FAVORITE QUOTE : "

WHAT IT INSPIRED ME TO?
(read/learn/visit)

"

3

BOOK TITLE :

AUTHOR :   **PAGES :**

PUBLISHER :   **PUB DATE :**

○ PAPERBACK   ○ HARDBACK   ○ E-BOOK   ○ AUDIOBOOK   ○ FICTION   ○ NON-FICTION

SOURCE :   ○ BOUGHT   ○ LOANED   FROM :

Genre :

Start Date :   *Finished Date* :

MY THOUGHTS :   *Rating* : ☆ ☆ ☆ ☆ ☆   *Ease of Reading* : ① ② ③ ④ ⑤

WHO WILL I RECOMMEND IT TO?

WHY I READ IT?

FAVORITE QUOTE : "

WHAT IT INSPIRED ME TO?
(read/learn/visit)

"

4

BOOK TITLE :

AUTHOR :   **PAGES :**

PUBLISHER :   **PUB DATE :**

○ PAPERBACK   ○ HARDBACK   ○ E-BOOK   ○ AUDIOBOOK   ○ FICTION   ○ NON-FICTION

SOURCE : ○ BOUGHT   ○ LOANED   **FROM :**

Genre :

Start Date :   *Finished Date :*

MY THOUGHTS :   *Rating :* ☆ ☆ ☆ ☆ ☆   *Ease of Reading :* ① ② ③ ④ ⑤

WHO WILL I RECOMMEND IT TO?

WHY I READ IT?

FAVORITE QUOTE : "

WHAT IT INSPIRED ME TO?
(read/learn/visit)

"

5

BOOK TITLE :

AUTHOR :   **PAGES :**

PUBLISHER :   **PUB DATE :**

○ PAPERBACK   ○ HARDBACK   ○ E-BOOK   ○ AUDIOBOOK   ○ FICTION   ○ NON-FICTION

SOURCE : ○ BOUGHT   ○ LOANED   **FROM :**

Genre :

Start Date :   *Finished Date* :

MY THOUGHTS :   *Rating :* ☆ ☆ ☆ ☆ ☆   *Ease of Reading :* ① ② ③ ④ ⑤

FAVORITE QUOTE : "

WHO WILL I RECOMMEND IT TO?

WHY I READ IT?

WHAT IT INSPIRED ME TO?
(read/learn/visit)

"

6

BOOK TITLE :

AUTHOR :   **PAGES :**

PUBLISHER :   **PUB DATE :**

○ PAPERBACK   ○ HARDBACK   ○ E-BOOK   ○ AUDIOBOOK   ○ FICTION   ○ NON-FICTION

SOURCE :   ○ BOUGHT   ○ LOANED   FROM :

Genre :

Start Date :   Finished Date :

MY THOUGHTS :   Rating : ☆ ☆ ☆ ☆ ☆   Ease of Reading : ① ② ③ ④ ⑤

WHO WILL I RECOMMEND IT TO?

WHY I READ IT?

FAVORITE QUOTE : "

WHAT IT INSPIRED ME TO?
(read/learn/visit)

"

7

BOOK TITLE :

AUTHOR :   **PAGES :**

PUBLISHER :   **PUB DATE :**

○ PAPERBACK   ○ HARDBACK   ○ E-BOOK   ○ AUDIOBOOK   ○ FICTION   ○ NON-FICTION

SOURCE :   ○ BOUGHT   ○ LOANED   FROM :

Genre :

Start Date :   *Finished Date* :

MY THOUGHTS :   *Rating :* ☆ ☆ ☆ ☆ ☆   *Ease of Reading :* ① ② ③ ④ ⑤

WHO WILL I RECOMMEND IT TO?

WHY I READ IT?

FAVORITE QUOTE : "

WHAT IT INSPIRED ME TO?
(read/learn/visit)

"

8

BOOK TITLE :

AUTHOR :   **PAGES :**

PUBLISHER :   **PUB DATE :**

○ PAPERBACK   ○ HARDBACK   ○ E-BOOK   ○ AUDIOBOOK   ○ FICTION   ○ NON-FICTION

SOURCE :   ○ BOUGHT   ○ LOANED   FROM :

Genre :

Start Date :   *Finished Date* :

MY THOUGHTS :   *Rating* : ☆ ☆ ☆ ☆ ☆   *Ease of Reading* : ① ② ③ ④ ⑤

WHO WILL I RECOMMEND IT TO?

WHY I READ IT?

FAVORITE QUOTE : "

WHAT IT INSPIRED ME TO?
(read/learn/visit)

"

9

BOOK TITLE : _____

AUTHOR : _____ **PAGES :** _____

PUBLISHER : _____ **PUB DATE :** _____

○ PAPERBACK ○ HARDBACK ○ E-BOOK ○ AUDIOBOOK ○ FICTION ○ NON-FICTION

SOURCE : ○ BOUGHT ○ LOANED **FROM :** _____

Genre : _____

Start Date : _____ _Finished Date_ : _____

MY THOUGHTS : _Rating_ : ☆ ☆ ☆ ☆ ☆ _Ease of Reading_ : ① ② ③ ④ ⑤

_____

_____

_____

_____

_____

_____

_____

_____

_____

_____

_____

_____

_____

_____

_____

_____

_____

_____

_____

WHO WILL I RECOMMEND IT TO?

WHY I READ IT?

FAVORITE QUOTE : "

WHAT IT INSPIRED ME TO?
(read/learn/visit)

"

10

BOOK TITLE :

AUTHOR :   **PAGES :**

PUBLISHER :   **PUB DATE :**

○ PAPERBACK   ○ HARDBACK   ○ E-BOOK   ○ AUDIOBOOK   ○ FICTION   ○ NON-FICTION

SOURCE :   ○ BOUGHT   ○ LOANED   **FROM :**

Genre :

Start Date :   *Finished Date* :

MY THOUGHTS :   *Rating* : ☆ ☆ ☆ ☆ ☆   *Ease of Reading* : ① ② ③ ④ ⑤

WHO WILL I RECOMMEND IT TO?

WHY I READ IT?

FAVORITE QUOTE : "

WHAT IT INSPIRED ME TO?
(read/learn/visit)

"

11

BOOK TITLE :

AUTHOR :   **PAGES :**

PUBLISHER :   **PUB DATE :**

○ PAPERBACK   ○ HARDBACK   ○ E-BOOK   ○ AUDIOBOOK   ○ FICTION   ○ NON-FICTION

SOURCE : ○ BOUGHT   ○ LOANED   **FROM :**

Genre :

Start Date :   *Finished Date :*

MY THOUGHTS :   *Rating :* ☆ ☆ ☆ ☆ ☆   *Ease of Reading :* ① ② ③ ④ ⑤

FAVORITE QUOTE : "

WHO WILL I RECOMMEND IT TO?

WHY I READ IT?

WHAT IT INSPIRED ME TO?
(read/learn/visit)

"

12

BOOK TITLE :

AUTHOR :   **PAGES :**

PUBLISHER :   **PUB DATE :**

○ PAPERBACK   ○ HARDBACK   ○ E-BOOK   ○ AUDIOBOOK   ○ FICTION   ○ NON-FICTION

SOURCE :   ○ BOUGHT   ○ LOANED   **FROM :**

Genre :

Start Date :   *Finished Date :*

MY THOUGHTS :   *Rating :* ☆ ☆ ☆ ☆ ☆   *Ease of Reading :* ① ② ③ ④ ⑤

WHO WILL I RECOMMEND IT TO?

WHY I READ IT?

FAVORITE QUOTE : "

WHAT IT INSPIRED ME TO?
(read/learn/visit)

"

13

BOOK TITLE :

AUTHOR :   **PAGES :**

PUBLISHER :   **PUB DATE :**

O PAPERBACK   O HARDBACK   O E-BOOK   O AUDIOBOOK   O FICTION   O NON-FICTION

SOURCE :   O BOUGHT   O LOANED   **FROM :**

Genre :

Start Date :   *Finished Date* :

MY THOUGHTS :   *Rating* : ☆ ☆ ☆ ☆ ☆   *Ease of Reading* : ① ② ③ ④ ⑤

WHO WILL I RECOMMEND IT TO?

WHY I READ IT?

FAVORITE QUOTE : "

WHAT IT INSPIRED ME TO?
(read/learn/visit)

"

14 BOOK TITLE : _____

AUTHOR : _____ PAGES : _____

PUBLISHER : _____ **PUB DATE :** _____

○ PAPERBACK   ○ HARDBACK   ○ E-BOOK   ○ AUDIOBOOK   ○ FICTION   ○ NON-FICTION

SOURCE :   ○ BOUGHT   ○ LOANED   **FROM :** _____

Genre : _____

Start Date : _____ *Finished Date :* _____

MY THOUGHTS :   *Rating :* ☆ ☆ ☆ ☆ ☆   *Ease of Reading :* ① ② ③ ④ ⑤

WHO WILL I RECOMMEND IT TO?

WHY I READ IT?

FAVORITE QUOTE : "

WHAT IT INSPIRED ME TO?
(read/learn/visit)

"

15

BOOK TITLE :

AUTHOR :   **PAGES :**

PUBLISHER :   **PUB DATE :**

O PAPERBACK   O HARDBACK   O E-BOOK   O AUDIOBOOK   O FICTION   O NON-FICTION

SOURCE :   O BOUGHT   O LOANED   FROM :

Genre :

Start Date :   *Finished Date :*

MY THOUGHTS :   *Rating :* ☆ ☆ ☆ ☆ ☆   *Ease of Reading :* ① ② ③ ④ ⑤

WHO WILL I RECOMMEND IT TO?

WHY I READ IT?

FAVORITE QUOTE : "

WHAT IT INSPIRED ME TO?
(read/learn/visit)

"

16

BOOK TITLE :

AUTHOR :   **PAGES :**

PUBLISHER :   **PUB DATE :**

○ PAPERBACK   ○ HARDBACK   ○ E-BOOK   ○ AUDIOBOOK   ○ FICTION   ○ NON-FICTION

SOURCE : ○ BOUGHT   ○ LOANED   FROM :

Genre :

Start Date :   *Finished Date* :

MY THOUGHTS :   *Rating* : ☆ ☆ ☆ ☆ ☆   *Ease of Reading* : ① ② ③ ④ ⑤

WHO WILL I RECOMMEND IT TO?

WHY I READ IT?

FAVORITE QUOTE : "

WHAT IT INSPIRED ME TO?
(read/learn/visit)

"

17 BOOK TITLE :

AUTHOR :   PAGES :

PUBLISHER :   **PUB DATE :**

○ PAPERBACK   ○ HARDBACK   ○ E-BOOK   ○ AUDIOBOOK   ○ FICTION   ○ NON-FICTION

SOURCE :   ○ BOUGHT   ○ LOANED   FROM :

Genre :

Start Date :   *Finished Date* :

MY THOUGHTS :   *Rating* : ☆ ☆ ☆ ☆ ☆   *Ease of Reading* : ① ② ③ ④ ⑤

WHO WILL I RECOMMEND IT TO?

WHY I READ IT?

FAVORITE QUOTE : "

WHAT IT INSPIRED ME TO?
(read/learn/visit)

"

18

BOOK TITLE : _____

AUTHOR : _____ **PAGES :** _____

PUBLISHER : _____ **PUB DATE :** _____

○ PAPERBACK ○ HARDBACK ○ E-BOOK ○ AUDIOBOOK ○ FICTION ○ NON-FICTION

SOURCE : ○ BOUGHT ○ LOANED **FROM :** _____

Genre : _____

Start Date : _____ _Finished Date_ : _____

MY THOUGHTS : _Rating_ : ☆ ☆ ☆ ☆ ☆ _Ease of Reading_ : ① ② ③ ④ ⑤

WHO WILL I RECOMMEND IT TO?

WHY I READ IT?

FAVORITE QUOTE : "

WHAT IT INSPIRED ME TO?
(read/learn/visit)

"

19

BOOK TITLE :

AUTHOR :   **PAGES :**

PUBLISHER :   **PUB DATE :**

○ PAPERBACK   ○ HARDBACK   ○ E-BOOK   ○ AUDIOBOOK   ○ FICTION   ○ NON-FICTION

SOURCE :   ○ BOUGHT   ○ LOANED   FROM :

Genre :

Start Date :   *Finished Date* :

MY THOUGHTS :   *Rating* : ☆ ☆ ☆ ☆ ☆   *Ease of Reading* : ① ② ③ ④ ⑤

FAVORITE QUOTE : "

WHO WILL I RECOMMEND IT TO?

WHY I READ IT?

WHAT IT INSPIRED ME TO?
(read/learn/visit)

"

20 BOOK TITLE :

AUTHOR :   PAGES :

PUBLISHER :   **PUB DATE :**

○ PAPERBACK   ○ HARDBACK   ○ E-BOOK   ○ AUDIOBOOK   ○ FICTION   ○ NON-FICTION

SOURCE : ○ BOUGHT   ○ LOANED   FROM :

Genre :

Start Date :   *Finished Date* :

MY THOUGHTS :   *Rating* : ☆ ☆ ☆ ☆ ☆   *Ease of Reading* : ① ② ③ ④ ⑤

WHO WILL I RECOMMEND IT TO?

WHY I READ IT?

FAVORITE QUOTE : "

WHAT IT INSPIRED ME TO?
(read/learn/visit)

"

21

BOOK TITLE :

AUTHOR :   **PAGES :**

PUBLISHER :   **PUB DATE :**

○ PAPERBACK   ○ HARDBACK   ○ E-BOOK   ○ AUDIOBOOK   ○ FICTION   ○ NON-FICTION

SOURCE : ○ BOUGHT   ○ LOANED   **FROM :**

Genre :

Start Date :   *Finished Date* :

MY THOUGHTS :   *Rating* : ☆ ☆ ☆ ☆ ☆   *Ease of Reading* : ① ② ③ ④ ⑤

WHO WILL I RECOMMEND IT TO?

WHY I READ IT?

FAVORITE QUOTE : "

WHAT IT INSPIRED ME TO?
(read/learn/visit)

"

22

BOOK TITLE :

AUTHOR :   **PAGES :**

PUBLISHER :   **PUB DATE :**

○ PAPERBACK   ○ HARDBACK   ○ E-BOOK   ○ AUDIOBOOK   ○ FICTION   ○ NON-FICTION

SOURCE :   ○ BOUGHT   ○ LOANED   **FROM :**

Genre :

Start Date :   *Finished Date :*

MY THOUGHTS :   *Rating :* ☆ ☆ ☆ ☆ ☆   *Ease of Reading :* ① ② ③ ④ ⑤

WHO WILL I RECOMMEND IT TO?

WHY I READ IT?

FAVORITE QUOTE : "

WHAT IT INSPIRED ME TO?
(*read/learn/visit*)

"

23

BOOK TITLE : _____

AUTHOR : _____ **PAGES :** _____

PUBLISHER : _____ **PUB DATE :** _____

○ PAPERBACK ○ HARDBACK ○ E-BOOK ○ AUDIOBOOK ○ FICTION ○ NON-FICTION

SOURCE : ○ BOUGHT ○ LOANED **FROM :** _____

Genre : _____

Start Date : _____ _Finished Date :_ _____

MY THOUGHTS : _Rating :_ ☆ ☆ ☆ ☆ ☆ _Ease of Reading :_ ① ② ③ ④ ⑤

_____

_____

_____

_____

_____

_____

_____

_____

_____

_____

_____

_____

_____

_____

_____

_____

WHO WILL I RECOMMEND IT TO?

WHY I READ IT?

FAVORITE QUOTE : "

WHAT IT INSPIRED ME TO?
(read/learn/visit)

"

24

BOOK TITLE :

AUTHOR :   **PAGES :**

PUBLISHER :   **PUB DATE :**

○ PAPERBACK   ○ HARDBACK   ○ E-BOOK   ○ AUDIOBOOK   ○ FICTION ○ NON-FICTION

SOURCE : ○ BOUGHT   ○ LOANED   FROM :

Genre :

Start Date :   *Finished Date* :

MY THOUGHTS :   *Rating :* ☆ ☆ ☆ ☆ ☆   *Ease of Reading :* ① ② ③ ④ ⑤

WHO WILL I RECOMMEND IT TO?

WHY I READ IT?

FAVORITE QUOTE : "

WHAT IT INSPIRED ME TO?
(read/learn/visit)

"

25 BOOK TITLE :

AUTHOR :

PAGES :

PUBLISHER :   PUB DATE :

○ PAPERBACK   ○ HARDBACK   ○ E-BOOK   ○ AUDIOBOOK   ○ FICTION   ○ NON-FICTION

SOURCE :   ○ BOUGHT   ○ LOANED   FROM :

Genre :

Start Date :   Finished Date :

MY THOUGHTS :   Rating : ☆ ☆ ☆ ☆ ☆   Ease of Reading : ① ② ③ ④ ⑤

WHO WILL I RECOMMEND IT TO?

WHY I READ IT?

FAVORITE QUOTE : "

WHAT IT INSPIRED ME TO?
(read/learn/visit)

"

Book Tracker

BOOK TITLE	AUTHOR	PAGE	DONE

26

BOOK TITLE :

AUTHOR :   **PAGES :**

PUBLISHER :   **PUB DATE :**

○ PAPERBACK   ○ HARDBACK   ○ E-BOOK   ○ AUDIOBOOK   ○ FICTION   ○ NON-FICTION

SOURCE :   ○ BOUGHT   ○ LOANED   **FROM :**

Genre :

Start Date :   *Finished Date* :

MY THOUGHTS :   *Rating* : ☆ ☆ ☆ ☆ ☆   *Ease of Reading* : ① ② ③ ④ ⑤

FAVORITE QUOTE : "

WHO WILL I RECOMMEND IT TO?

WHY I READ IT?

WHAT IT INSPIRED ME TO?
(read/learn/visit)

27

BOOK TITLE :

AUTHOR :   **PAGES :**

PUBLISHER :   **PUB DATE :**

○ PAPERBACK   ○ HARDBACK   ○ E-BOOK   ○ AUDIOBOOK   ○ FICTION   ○ NON-FICTION

SOURCE : ○ BOUGHT   ○ LOANED   **FROM :**

Genre :

Start Date :   *Finished Date :*

MY THOUGHTS :   *Rating :* ☆ ☆ ☆ ☆ ☆   *Ease of Reading :* ① ② ③ ④ ⑤

WHO WILL I RECOMMEND IT TO?

WHY I READ IT?

FAVORITE QUOTE : "

WHAT IT INSPIRED ME TO?
(read/learn/visit)

"

28 BOOK TITLE :

AUTHOR :   PAGES :

PUBLISHER :   PUB DATE :

○ PAPERBACK ○ HARDBACK ○ E-BOOK ○ AUDIOBOOK   ○ FICTION ○ NON-FICTION

SOURCE : ○ BOUGHT   ○ LOANED   FROM :

Genre :

Start Date :   Finished Date :

MY THOUGHTS :   Rating : ☆ ☆ ☆ ☆ ☆   Ease of Reading : ① ② ③ ④ ⑤

FAVORITE QUOTE : "

WHO WILL I RECOMMEND IT TO?

WHY I READ IT?

WHAT IT INSPIRED ME TO?
(read/learn/visit)

"

29 BOOK TITLE :

AUTHOR :

PAGES :

PUBLISHER :

PUB DATE :

○ PAPERBACK   ○ HARDBACK   ○ E-BOOK   ○ AUDIOBOOK   ○ FICTION   ○ NON-FICTION

SOURCE :   ○ BOUGHT   ○ LOANED   FROM :

Genre :

Start Date :   Finished Date :

MY THOUGHTS :   Rating : ☆ ☆ ☆ ☆ ☆   Ease of Reading : ① ② ③ ④ ⑤

WHO WILL I RECOMMEND IT TO?

WHY I READ IT?

FAVORITE QUOTE : "

WHAT IT INSPIRED ME TO?
(read/learn/visit)

"

30 BOOK TITLE :

AUTHOR :   PAGES :

PUBLISHER :   **PUB DATE :**

○ PAPERBACK   ○ HARDBACK   ○ E-BOOK   ○ AUDIOBOOK   ○ FICTION   ○ NON-FICTION

SOURCE : ○ BOUGHT   ○ LOANED   FROM :

Genre :

Start Date :   Finished Date :

MY THOUGHTS :   Rating : ☆ ☆ ☆ ☆ ☆   Ease of Reading : ① ② ③ ④ ⑤

WHO WILL I RECOMMEND IT TO?

WHY I READ IT?

FAVORITE QUOTE : "

WHAT IT INSPIRED ME TO?
(read/learn/visit)

"

31

BOOK TITLE :

AUTHOR :   **PAGES :**

PUBLISHER :   **PUB DATE :**

○ PAPERBACK   ○ HARDBACK   ○ E-BOOK   ○ AUDIOBOOK   ○ FICTION   ○ NON-FICTION

SOURCE : ○ BOUGHT   ○ LOANED   **FROM :**

Genre :

Start Date :   *Finished Date :*

MY THOUGHTS :   *Rating :* ☆ ☆ ☆ ☆ ☆   *Ease of Reading :* ① ② ③ ④ ⑤

WHO WILL I RECOMMEND IT TO?

WHY I READ IT?

FAVORITE QUOTE : "

WHAT IT INSPIRED ME TO?
(read/learn/visit)

"

32

BOOK TITLE :

AUTHOR :   **PAGES :**

PUBLISHER :   **PUB DATE :**

○ PAPERBACK   ○ HARDBACK   ○ E-BOOK   ○ AUDIOBOOK   ○ FICTION   ○ NON-FICTION

SOURCE :   ○ BOUGHT   ○ LOANED   **FROM :**

Genre :

Start Date :   *Finished Date* :

MY THOUGHTS :   *Rating* : ☆ ☆ ☆ ☆ ☆   *Ease of Reading* : ① ② ③ ④ ⑤

WHO WILL I RECOMMEND IT TO?

WHY I READ IT?

FAVORITE QUOTE : ❝

WHAT IT INSPIRED ME TO?
(read/learn/visit)

❞

33 BOOK TITLE :

AUTHOR :   PAGES :

PUBLISHER :   **PUB DATE :**

○ PAPERBACK   ○ HARDBACK   ○ E-BOOK   ○ AUDIOBOOK   ○ FICTION   ○ NON-FICTION

SOURCE : ○ BOUGHT   ○ LOANED   **FROM :**

Genre :

Start Date :   *Finished Date* :

MY THOUGHTS :   *Rating* : ☆ ☆ ☆ ☆ ☆   *Ease of Reading* : ① ② ③ ④ ⑤

WHO WILL I RECOMMEND IT TO?

WHY I READ IT?

FAVORITE QUOTE : "

WHAT IT INSPIRED ME TO?
(read/learn/visit)

"

34

BOOK TITLE :

AUTHOR :   **PAGES :**

PUBLISHER :   **PUB DATE :**

○ PAPERBACK   ○ HARDBACK   ○ E-BOOK   ○ AUDIOBOOK   ○ FICTION   ○ NON-FICTION

SOURCE : ○ BOUGHT   ○ LOANED   **FROM :**

Genre :

Start Date :   *Finished Date* :

MY THOUGHTS :   *Rating* : ☆ ☆ ☆ ☆ ☆   *Ease of Reading* : ① ② ③ ④ ⑤

WHO WILL I RECOMMEND IT TO?

WHY I READ IT?

FAVORITE QUOTE : "

WHAT IT INSPIRED ME TO?
(read/learn/visit)

"

35 BOOK TITLE :

AUTHOR :   PAGES :

PUBLISHER :   PUB DATE :

○ PAPERBACK   ○ HARDBACK   ○ E-BOOK   ○ AUDIOBOOK   ○ FICTION   ○ NON-FICTION

SOURCE :   ○ BOUGHT   ○ LOANED   FROM :

Genre :

Start Date :   *Finished Date* :

MY THOUGHTS :   *Rating* : ☆ ☆ ☆ ☆ ☆   *Ease of Reading* : ① ② ③ ④ ⑤

WHO WILL I RECOMMEND IT TO?

WHY I READ IT?

FAVORITE QUOTE : "

WHAT IT INSPIRED ME TO?
(read/learn/visit)

"

36

BOOK TITLE :

AUTHOR : **PAGES :**

PUBLISHER : **PUB DATE :**

○ PAPERBACK ○ HARDBACK ○ E-BOOK ○ AUDIOBOOK ○ FICTION ○ NON-FICTION

SOURCE : ○ BOUGHT ○ LOANED **FROM :**

Genre :

Start Date : *Finished Date :*

MY THOUGHTS : *Rating :* ☆ ☆ ☆ ☆ ☆ *Ease of Reading :* ① ② ③ ④ ⑤

FAVORITE QUOTE : "

WHO WILL I RECOMMEND IT TO?

WHY I READ IT?

WHAT IT INSPIRED ME TO?
(read/learn/visit)

37

BOOK TITLE :

AUTHOR :   **PAGES :**

PUBLISHER :   **PUB DATE :**

○ PAPERBACK   ○ HARDBACK   ○ E-BOOK   ○ AUDIOBOOK   ○ FICTION   ○ NON-FICTION

SOURCE :   ○ BOUGHT   ○ LOANED   **FROM :**

Genre :

Start Date :   *Finished Date* :

MY THOUGHTS :   *Rating* : ☆ ☆ ☆ ☆ ☆   *Ease of Reading* : ① ② ③ ④ ⑤

WHO WILL I RECOMMEND IT TO?

WHY I READ IT?

FAVORITE QUOTE : "

WHAT IT INSPIRED ME TO?
(read/learn/visit)

"

38

BOOK TITLE :

AUTHOR :   **PAGES :**

PUBLISHER :   **PUB DATE :**

○ PAPERBACK   ○ HARDBACK   ○ E-BOOK   ○ AUDIOBOOK   ○ FICTION   ○ NON-FICTION

SOURCE :   ○ BOUGHT   ○ LOANED   FROM :

Genre :

Start Date :   *Finished Date* :

MY THOUGHTS :   *Rating* : ☆ ☆ ☆ ☆ ☆   *Ease of Reading* : ① ② ③ ④ ⑤

WHO WILL I RECOMMEND IT TO?

WHY I READ IT?

FAVORITE QUOTE : "

WHAT IT INSPIRED ME TO?
(read/learn/visit)

"

39

BOOK TITLE :

AUTHOR :   **PAGES :**

PUBLISHER :   **PUB DATE :**

○ PAPERBACK   ○ HARDBACK   ○ E-BOOK   ○ AUDIOBOOK   ○ FICTION   ○ NON-FICTION

SOURCE :   ○ BOUGHT   ○ LOANED   **FROM :**

Genre :

Start Date :   *Finished Date* :

MY THOUGHTS :   *Rating* : ☆ ☆ ☆ ☆ ☆   *Ease of Reading* : ① ② ③ ④ ⑤

WHO WILL I RECOMMEND IT TO?

WHY I READ IT?

FAVORITE QUOTE : "

WHAT IT INSPIRED ME TO?
(read/learn/visit)

"

40

BOOK TITLE :

AUTHOR :   **PAGES :**

PUBLISHER :   **PUB DATE :**

○ PAPERBACK   ○ HARDBACK   ○ E-BOOK   ○ AUDIOBOOK   ○ FICTION   ○ NON-FICTION

SOURCE :   ○ BOUGHT   ○ LOANED   **FROM :**

Genre :

Start Date :   *Finished Date* :

MY THOUGHTS :   *Rating* : ☆ ☆ ☆ ☆ ☆   *Ease of Reading* : ① ② ③ ④ ⑤

WHO WILL I RECOMMEND IT TO?

WHY I READ IT?

FAVORITE QUOTE : "

WHAT IT INSPIRED ME TO?
(read/learn/visit)

"

41

BOOK TITLE :

AUTHOR :   **PAGES :**

PUBLISHER :   **PUB DATE :**

○ PAPERBACK   ○ HARDBACK   ○ E-BOOK   ○ AUDIOBOOK   ○ FICTION   ○ NON-FICTION

SOURCE :   ○ BOUGHT   ○ LOANED   FROM :

Genre :

Start Date :   *Finished Date :*

MY THOUGHTS :   *Rating :* ☆ ☆ ☆ ☆ ☆   *Ease of Reading :* ① ② ③ ④ ⑤

WHO WILL I RECOMMEND IT TO?

WHY I READ IT?

FAVORITE QUOTE : "

WHAT IT INSPIRED ME TO?
(read/learn/visit)

"

42

BOOK TITLE : _____

AUTHOR : _____ **PAGES :** _____

PUBLISHER : _____ **PUB DATE :** _____

○ PAPERBACK ○ HARDBACK ○ E-BOOK ○ AUDIOBOOK ○ FICTION ○ NON-FICTION

SOURCE : ○ BOUGHT ○ LOANED **FROM :** _____

Genre : _____

Start Date : _____ _Finished Date_ : _____

MY THOUGHTS : _Rating_ : ☆ ☆ ☆ ☆ ☆ _Ease of Reading_ : ① ② ③ ④ ⑤

_____

_____

_____

_____

_____

_____

_____

_____

_____

_____

_____

_____

_____

_____

WHO WILL I RECOMMEND IT TO?

WHY I READ IT?

FAVORITE QUOTE : "

WHAT IT INSPIRED ME TO?
(read/learn/visit)

"

43

BOOK TITLE :

AUTHOR :   **PAGES :**

PUBLISHER :   **PUB DATE :**

○ PAPERBACK   ○ HARDBACK   ○ E-BOOK   ○ AUDIOBOOK   ○ FICTION   ○ NON-FICTION

SOURCE :   ○ BOUGHT   ○ LOANED   FROM :

Genre :

Start Date :   *Finished Date* :

MY THOUGHTS :   *Rating* : ☆ ☆ ☆ ☆ ☆   *Ease of Reading* : ① ② ③ ④ ⑤

WHO WILL I RECOMMEND IT TO?

WHY I READ IT?

FAVORITE QUOTE : "

WHAT IT INSPIRED ME TO?
(*read/learn/visit*)

"

44 BOOK TITLE :

AUTHOR :   PAGES :

PUBLISHER :   PUB DATE :

○ PAPERBACK   ○ HARDBACK   ○ E-BOOK   ○ AUDIOBOOK   ○ FICTION   ○ NON-FICTION

SOURCE :   ○ BOUGHT   ○ LOANED   FROM :

Genre :

Start Date :   Finished Date :

MY THOUGHTS :   Rating : ☆ ☆ ☆ ☆ ☆   Ease of Reading : ① ② ③ ④ ⑤

WHO WILL I RECOMMEND IT TO?

WHY I READ IT?

FAVORITE QUOTE : "

WHAT IT INSPIRED ME TO?
(read/learn/visit)

"

45

BOOK TITLE :

AUTHOR :   **PAGES :**

PUBLISHER :   **PUB DATE :**

○ PAPERBACK   ○ HARDBACK   ○ E-BOOK   ○ AUDIOBOOK   ○ FICTION   ○ NON-FICTION

SOURCE :   ○ BOUGHT   ○ LOANED   **FROM :**

Genre :

Start Date :   *Finished Date* :

MY THOUGHTS :   *Rating :* ☆ ☆ ☆ ☆ ☆   *Ease of Reading :* ① ② ③ ④ ⑤

WHO WILL I RECOMMEND IT TO?

WHY I READ IT?

FAVORITE QUOTE : "

WHAT IT INSPIRED ME TO?
(read/learn/visit)

"

46

BOOK TITLE :

AUTHOR :   **PAGES :**

PUBLISHER :   **PUB DATE :**

○ PAPERBACK   ○ HARDBACK   ○ E-BOOK   ○ AUDIOBOOK   ○ FICTION   ○ NON-FICTION

SOURCE :   ○ BOUGHT   ○ LOANED   FROM :

Genre :

Start Date :   *Finished Date* :

MY THOUGHTS :   *Rating* : ☆ ☆ ☆ ☆ ☆   *Ease of Reading* : ① ② ③ ④ ⑤

WHO WILL I RECOMMEND IT TO?

WHY I READ IT?

FAVORITE QUOTE : "

WHAT IT INSPIRED ME TO?
(read/learn/visit)

"

47

BOOK TITLE :

AUTHOR :   **PAGES :**

PUBLISHER :   **PUB DATE :**

○ PAPERBACK   ○ HARDBACK   ○ E-BOOK   ○ AUDIOBOOK   ○ FICTION   ○ NON-FICTION

SOURCE :   ○ BOUGHT   ○ LOANED   **FROM :**

Genre :

Start Date :   *Finished Date :*

MY THOUGHTS :   *Rating :* ☆ ☆ ☆ ☆ ☆   *Ease of Reading :* ① ② ③ ④ ⑤

WHO WILL I RECOMMEND IT TO?

WHY I READ IT?

FAVORITE QUOTE : "

WHAT IT INSPIRED ME TO?
(read/learn/visit)

"

48

BOOK TITLE :

AUTHOR :   **PAGES :**

PUBLISHER :   **PUB DATE :**

○ PAPERBACK   ○ HARDBACK   ○ E-BOOK   ○ AUDIOBOOK   ○ FICTION ○ NON-FICTION

SOURCE : ○ BOUGHT   ○ LOANED   FROM :

Genre :

Start Date :   *Finished Date* :

MY THOUGHTS :   *Rating* : ☆ ☆ ☆ ☆ ☆   *Ease of Reading* : ① ② ③ ④ ⑤

WHO WILL I RECOMMEND IT TO?

WHY I READ IT?

FAVORITE QUOTE : "

WHAT IT INSPIRED ME TO?
(read/learn/visit)

"

49 BOOK TITLE :

AUTHOR :   PAGES :

PUBLISHER :   **PUB DATE :**

○ PAPERBACK   ○ HARDBACK   ○ E-BOOK   ○ AUDIOBOOK   ○ FICTION   ○ NON-FICTION

SOURCE :   ○ BOUGHT   ○ LOANED   FROM :

Genre :

Start Date :   Finished Date :

MY THOUGHTS :   Rating : ☆ ☆ ☆ ☆ ☆   Ease of Reading : ① ② ③ ④ ⑤

WHO WILL I RECOMMEND IT TO?

WHY I READ IT?

FAVORITE QUOTE : "

WHAT IT INSPIRED ME TO?
(read/learn/visit)

"

50

BOOK TITLE :

AUTHOR :   **PAGES :**

PUBLISHER :   **PUB DATE :**

○ PAPERBACK   ○ HARDBACK   ○ E-BOOK   ○ AUDIOBOOK   ○ FICTION   ○ NON-FICTION

SOURCE :   ○ BOUGHT   ○ LOANED   FROM :

Genre :

Start Date :   *Finished Date* :

MY THOUGHTS :   *Rating* : ☆ ☆ ☆ ☆ ☆   *Ease of Reading* : ① ② ③ ④ ⑤

WHO WILL I RECOMMEND IT TO?

WHY I READ IT?

FAVORITE QUOTE : "

WHAT IT INSPIRED ME TO?
(read/learn/visit)

"

Book Tracker

BOOK TITLE	AUTHOR	PAGE	DONE

51

BOOK TITLE :

AUTHOR :   **PAGES :**

PUBLISHER :   **PUB DATE :**

○ PAPERBACK   ○ HARDBACK   ○ E-BOOK   ○ AUDIOBOOK   ○ FICTION   ○ NON-FICTION

SOURCE :   ○ BOUGHT   ○ LOANED   **FROM :**

Genre :

Start Date :   *Finished Date :*

MY THOUGHTS :   *Rating :* ☆☆☆☆☆   *Ease of Reading :* ① ② ③ ④ ⑤

WHO WILL I RECOMMEND IT TO?

WHY I READ IT?

FAVORITE QUOTE : "

WHAT IT INSPIRED ME TO?
(read/learn/visit)

"

52

BOOK TITLE :

AUTHOR :   **PAGES :**

PUBLISHER :   **PUB DATE :**

○ PAPERBACK   ○ HARDBACK   ○ E-BOOK   ○ AUDIOBOOK   ○ FICTION   ○ NON-FICTION

SOURCE :   ○ BOUGHT   ○ LOANED   **FROM :**

Genre :

Start Date :   *Finished Date* :

MY THOUGHTS :   *Rating :* ☆ ☆ ☆ ☆ ☆   *Ease of Reading :* ① ② ③ ④ ⑤

WHO WILL I RECOMMEND IT TO?

WHY I READ IT?

FAVORITE QUOTE : "

WHAT IT INSPIRED ME TO?
(read/learn/visit)

"

53

BOOK TITLE : _____

AUTHOR : _____ **PAGES :** _____

PUBLISHER : _____ **PUB DATE :** _____

○ PAPERBACK ○ HARDBACK ○ E-BOOK ○ AUDIOBOOK ○ FICTION ○ NON-FICTION

SOURCE : ○ BOUGHT ○ LOANED **FROM :** _____

Genre : _____

Start Date : _____ _Finished Date :_ _____

MY THOUGHTS : _Rating :_ ☆ ☆ ☆ ☆ ☆   _Ease of Reading :_ ① ② ③ ④ ⑤

FAVORITE QUOTE : "

WHO WILL I RECOMMEND IT TO?

WHY I READ IT?

WHAT IT INSPIRED ME TO?
(read/learn/visit)

"

54

BOOK TITLE :

AUTHOR :   **PAGES :**

PUBLISHER :   **PUB DATE :**

○ PAPERBACK   ○ HARDBACK   ○ E-BOOK   ○ AUDIOBOOK   ○ FICTION   ○ NON-FICTION

SOURCE : ○ BOUGHT   ○ LOANED   **FROM :**

Genre :

Start Date :   *Finished Date :*

MY THOUGHTS :   *Rating :* ☆ ☆ ☆ ☆ ☆   *Ease of Reading :* ① ② ③ ④ ⑤

WHO WILL I RECOMMEND IT TO?

WHY I READ IT?

FAVORITE QUOTE : "

WHAT IT INSPIRED ME TO?
(read/learn/visit)

"

55

BOOK TITLE :

AUTHOR :   **PAGES :**

PUBLISHER :   **PUB DATE :**

○ PAPERBACK   ○ HARDBACK   ○ E-BOOK   ○ AUDIOBOOK   ○ FICTION   ○ NON-FICTION

SOURCE :   ○ BOUGHT   ○ LOANED   FROM :

Genre :

Start Date :   *Finished Date* :

MY THOUGHTS :   *Rating* : ☆ ☆ ☆ ☆ ☆   *Ease of Reading* : ① ② ③ ④ ⑤

WHO WILL I RECOMMEND IT TO?

WHY I READ IT?

FAVORITE QUOTE : "

WHAT IT INSPIRED ME TO?
(read/learn/visit)

"

56

BOOK TITLE :

AUTHOR :   **PAGES :**

PUBLISHER :   **PUB DATE :**

○ PAPERBACK   ○ HARDBACK   ○ E-BOOK   ○ AUDIOBOOK   ○ FICTION   ○ NON-FICTION

SOURCE : ○ BOUGHT   ○ LOANED   **FROM :**

Genre :

Start Date :   *Finished Date :*

MY THOUGHTS :   *Rating :* ☆☆☆☆☆   *Ease of Reading :* ① ② ③ ④ ⑤

WHO WILL I RECOMMEND IT TO?

WHY I READ IT?

FAVORITE QUOTE : "

WHAT IT INSPIRED ME TO?
(read/learn/visit)

"

57

BOOK TITLE : _____

AUTHOR : _____ **PAGES :** _____

PUBLISHER : _____ **PUB DATE :** _____

○ PAPERBACK ○ HARDBACK ○ E-BOOK ○ AUDIOBOOK ○ FICTION ○ NON-FICTION

SOURCE : ○ BOUGHT ○ LOANED **FROM :** _____

Genre : _____

Start Date : _____ _Finished Date_ : _____

MY THOUGHTS : _Rating_ : ☆ ☆ ☆ ☆ ☆ _Ease of Reading_ : ① ② ③ ④ ⑤

_____

_____

_____

_____

_____

_____

_____

_____

_____

_____

_____

_____

_____

_____

WHO WILL I RECOMMEND IT TO?

_____

WHY I READ IT?

FAVORITE QUOTE : "

WHAT IT INSPIRED ME TO?
(read/learn/visit)

"

58 BOOK TITLE :

AUTHOR : _____ PAGES : _____

PUBLISHER : _____ PUB DATE : _____

○ PAPERBACK ○ HARDBACK ○ E-BOOK ○ AUDIOBOOK ○ FICTION ○ NON-FICTION

SOURCE : ○ BOUGHT ○ LOANED FROM : _____

Genre : _____

Start Date : _____ *Finished Date* : _____

MY THOUGHTS : *Rating* : ☆ ☆ ☆ ☆ ☆ *Ease of Reading* : ① ② ③ ④ ⑤

WHO WILL I RECOMMEND IT TO?

WHY I READ IT?

FAVORITE QUOTE : "

WHAT IT INSPIRED ME TO?
(read/learn/visit)

"

59 BOOK TITLE :

AUTHOR :   PAGES :

PUBLISHER :   PUB DATE :

○ PAPERBACK   ○ HARDBACK   ○ E-BOOK   ○ AUDIOBOOK   ○ FICTION   ○ NON-FICTION

SOURCE : ○ BOUGHT   ○ LOANED   FROM :

Genre :

Start Date :   Finished Date :

MY THOUGHTS :   Rating : ☆ ☆ ☆ ☆ ☆   Ease of Reading : ① ② ③ ④ ⑤

WHO WILL I RECOMMEND IT TO?

WHY I READ IT?

FAVORITE QUOTE : "

WHAT IT INSPIRED ME TO?
(read/learn/visit)

"

60

BOOK TITLE :

AUTHOR :   **PAGES :**

PUBLISHER :   **PUB DATE :**

○ PAPERBACK   ○ HARDBACK   ○ E-BOOK   ○ AUDIOBOOK   ○ FICTION   ○ NON-FICTION

SOURCE :   ○ BOUGHT   ○ LOANED   FROM :

Genre :

Start Date :   *Finished Date* :

MY THOUGHTS :   *Rating* : ☆ ☆ ☆ ☆ ☆   *Ease of Reading* : ① ② ③ ④ ⑤

WHO WILL I RECOMMEND IT TO?

WHY I READ IT?

FAVORITE QUOTE : "

WHAT IT INSPIRED ME TO?
(read/learn/visit)

"

61

BOOK TITLE : _____

AUTHOR : _____ **PAGES :** _____

PUBLISHER : _____ **PUB DATE :** _____

○ PAPERBACK ○ HARDBACK ○ E-BOOK ○ AUDIOBOOK ○ FICTION ○ NON-FICTION

SOURCE : ○ BOUGHT ○ LOANED **FROM :** _____

Genre : _____

Start Date : _____ *Finished Date :* _____

MY THOUGHTS : *Rating :* ☆ ☆ ☆ ☆ ☆ *Ease of Reading :* ① ② ③ ④ ⑤

_____
_____
_____
_____
_____
_____
_____
_____
_____
_____
_____
_____
_____
_____
_____

WHO WILL I RECOMMEND IT TO?

WHY I READ IT?

FAVORITE QUOTE : "

WHAT IT INSPIRED ME TO?
(read/learn/visit)

"

62

BOOK TITLE :

AUTHOR :   **PAGES :**

PUBLISHER :   **PUB DATE :**

○ PAPERBACK   ○ HARDBACK   ○ E-BOOK   ○ AUDIOBOOK   ○ FICTION   ○ NON-FICTION

SOURCE : ○ BOUGHT   ○ LOANED   FROM :

Genre :

Start Date :   *Finished Date* :

MY THOUGHTS :   *Rating :* ☆ ☆ ☆ ☆ ☆   *Ease of Reading :* ① ② ③ ④ ⑤

WHO WILL I RECOMMEND IT TO?

WHY I READ IT?

FAVORITE QUOTE : "

WHAT IT INSPIRED ME TO?
(read/learn/visit)

"

63

BOOK TITLE :

AUTHOR : **PAGES :**

PUBLISHER : **PUB DATE :**

○ PAPERBACK ○ HARDBACK ○ E-BOOK ○ AUDIOBOOK ○ FICTION ○ NON-FICTION

SOURCE : ○ BOUGHT ○ LOANED **FROM :**

Genre :

Start Date : *Finished Date* :

MY THOUGHTS : *Rating :* ☆☆☆☆☆ *Ease of Reading :* ①②③④⑤

WHO WILL I RECOMMEND IT TO?

WHY I READ IT?

FAVORITE QUOTE : "

WHAT IT INSPIRED ME TO?
(read/learn/visit)

"

64

BOOK TITLE :

AUTHOR :   **PAGES :**

PUBLISHER :   **PUB DATE :**

○ PAPERBACK   ○ HARDBACK   ○ E-BOOK   ○ AUDIOBOOK   ○ FICTION   ○ NON-FICTION

SOURCE :   ○ BOUGHT   ○ LOANED   **FROM :**

Genre :

Start Date :   *Finished Date :*

MY THOUGHTS :   *Rating :* ☆ ☆ ☆ ☆ ☆   *Ease of Reading :* ① ② ③ ④ ⑤

WHO WILL I RECOMMEND IT TO?

WHY I READ IT?

FAVORITE QUOTE : "

WHAT IT INSPIRED ME TO?
(read/learn/visit)

"

65

BOOK TITLE : _____

AUTHOR : _____ **PAGES :** _____

PUBLISHER : _____ **PUB DATE :** _____

○ PAPERBACK   ○ HARDBACK   ○ E-BOOK   ○ AUDIOBOOK   ○ FICTION   ○ NON-FICTION

SOURCE :   ○ BOUGHT   ○ LOANED   **FROM :** _____

Genre : _____

Start Date : _____ *Finished Date :* _____

MY THOUGHTS :   *Rating :* ☆ ☆ ☆ ☆ ☆   *Ease of Reading :* ① ② ③ ④ ⑤

_____
_____
_____
_____
_____
_____
_____
_____
_____
_____
_____
_____
_____
_____
_____
_____
_____

WHO WILL I RECOMMEND IT TO?

WHY I READ IT?

FAVORITE QUOTE : "

WHAT IT INSPIRED ME TO?
(read/learn/visit)

"

66 BOOK TITLE :

AUTHOR :   PAGES :

PUBLISHER :   PUB DATE :

○ PAPERBACK   ○ HARDBACK   ○ E-BOOK   ○ AUDIOBOOK   ○ FICTION   ○ NON-FICTION

SOURCE : ○ BOUGHT   ○ LOANED   FROM :

Genre :

Start Date :   Finished Date :

MY THOUGHTS :   Rating : ☆ ☆ ☆ ☆ ☆   Ease of Reading : ① ② ③ ④ ⑤

WHO WILL I RECOMMEND IT TO?

WHY I READ IT?

FAVORITE QUOTE : "

WHAT IT INSPIRED ME TO?
(read/learn/visit)

"

67

BOOK TITLE :

AUTHOR :   **PAGES :**

PUBLISHER :   **PUB DATE :**

○ PAPERBACK   ○ HARDBACK   ○ E-BOOK   ○ AUDIOBOOK   ○ FICTION   ○ NON-FICTION

SOURCE : ○ BOUGHT   ○ LOANED   **FROM :**

Genre :

Start Date :   *Finished Date :*

MY THOUGHTS :   *Rating :* ☆ ☆ ☆ ☆ ☆   *Ease of Reading :* ① ② ③ ④ ⑤

FAVORITE QUOTE : "

WHO WILL I RECOMMEND IT TO?

WHY I READ IT?

WHAT IT INSPIRED ME TO?
(read/learn/visit)

68

BOOK TITLE :

AUTHOR :   **PAGES :**

PUBLISHER :   **PUB DATE :**

○ PAPERBACK   ○ HARDBACK   ○ E-BOOK   ○ AUDIOBOOK   ○ FICTION   ○ NON-FICTION

SOURCE :   ○ BOUGHT   ○ LOANED   **FROM :**

Genre :

Start Date :   *Finished Date* :

MY THOUGHTS :   *Rating* : ☆ ☆ ☆ ☆ ☆   *Ease of Reading* : ① ② ③ ④ ⑤

WHO WILL I RECOMMEND IT TO?

WHY I READ IT?

FAVORITE QUOTE : "

WHAT IT INSPIRED ME TO?
(read/learn/visit)

"

69

BOOK TITLE :

AUTHOR :   **PAGES :**

PUBLISHER :   **PUB DATE :**

○ PAPERBACK ○ HARDBACK ○ E-BOOK ○ AUDIOBOOK   ○ FICTION ○ NON-FICTION

SOURCE : ○ BOUGHT   ○ LOANED   **FROM :**

Genre :

Start Date :   *Finished Date :*

MY THOUGHTS :   *Rating :* ☆ ☆ ☆ ☆ ☆   *Ease of Reading :* ① ② ③ ④ ⑤

FAVORITE QUOTE : "

WHO WILL I RECOMMEND IT TO?

WHY I READ IT?

WHAT IT INSPIRED ME TO?
(read/learn/visit)

70

BOOK TITLE :

AUTHOR :   **PAGES :**

PUBLISHER :   **PUB DATE :**

○ PAPERBACK   ○ HARDBACK   ○ E-BOOK   ○ AUDIOBOOK   ○ FICTION   ○ NON-FICTION

SOURCE :   ○ BOUGHT   ○ LOANED   FROM :

Genre :

Start Date :   *Finished Date* :

MY THOUGHTS :   *Rating* : ☆ ☆ ☆ ☆ ☆   *Ease of Reading* : ① ② ③ ④ ⑤

WHO WILL I RECOMMEND IT TO?

WHY I READ IT?

FAVORITE QUOTE : "

WHAT IT INSPIRED ME TO?
(read/learn/visit)

"

71

BOOK TITLE :

AUTHOR :   **PAGES :**

PUBLISHER :   **PUB DATE :**

○ PAPERBACK   ○ HARDBACK   ○ E-BOOK   ○ AUDIOBOOK   ○ FICTION   ○ NON-FICTION

SOURCE :   ○ BOUGHT   ○ LOANED   FROM :

Genre :

Start Date :   *Finished Date* :

MY THOUGHTS :   *Rating* : ☆ ☆ ☆ ☆ ☆   *Ease of Reading* : ① ② ③ ④ ⑤

WHO WILL I RECOMMEND IT TO?

WHY I READ IT?

FAVORITE QUOTE : ❝

WHAT IT INSPIRED ME TO?
(read/learn/visit)

❞

72

BOOK TITLE :

AUTHOR :   **PAGES :**

PUBLISHER :   **PUB DATE :**

○ PAPERBACK   ○ HARDBACK   ○ E-BOOK   ○ AUDIOBOOK   ○ FICTION   ○ NON-FICTION

SOURCE :   ○ BOUGHT   ○ LOANED   **FROM :**

Genre :

Start Date :   *Finished Date* :

MY THOUGHTS :   *Rating* : ☆ ☆ ☆ ☆ ☆   *Ease of Reading* : ① ② ③ ④ ⑤

WHO WILL I RECOMMEND IT TO?

WHY I READ IT?

FAVORITE QUOTE : "

WHAT IT INSPIRED ME TO?
(read/learn/visit)

"

73 BOOK TITLE :

AUTHOR :   **PAGES :**

PUBLISHER :   **PUB DATE :**

○ PAPERBACK   ○ HARDBACK   ○ E-BOOK   ○ AUDIOBOOK   ○ FICTION   ○ NON-FICTION

SOURCE :   ○ BOUGHT   ○ LOANED   FROM :

Genre :

Start Date :   *Finished Date* :

MY THOUGHTS :   *Rating* : ☆ ☆ ☆ ☆ ☆   *Ease of Reading* : ① ② ③ ④ ⑤

FAVORITE QUOTE : "

WHO WILL I RECOMMEND IT TO?

WHY I READ IT?

WHAT IT INSPIRED ME TO?
(read/learn/visit)

"

74

BOOK TITLE :

AUTHOR :   **PAGES :**

PUBLISHER :   **PUB DATE :**

○ PAPERBACK   ○ HARDBACK   ○ E-BOOK   ○ AUDIOBOOK   ○ FICTION   ○ NON-FICTION

SOURCE : ○ BOUGHT   ○ LOANED   **FROM :**

Genre :

Start Date :   *Finished Date :*

MY THOUGHTS :   *Rating :* ☆ ☆ ☆ ☆ ☆   *Ease of Reading :* ① ② ③ ④ ⑤

WHO WILL I RECOMMEND IT TO?

WHY I READ IT?

FAVORITE QUOTE : "

WHAT IT INSPIRED ME TO?
(read/learn/visit)

"

75

BOOK TITLE :

AUTHOR :   **PAGES :**

PUBLISHER :   **PUB DATE :**

○ PAPERBACK   ○ HARDBACK   ○ E-BOOK   ○ AUDIOBOOK   ○ FICTION   ○ NON-FICTION

SOURCE : ○ BOUGHT   ○ LOANED   FROM :

Genre :

Start Date :   *Finished Date* :

MY THOUGHTS :   *Rating :* ☆ ☆ ☆ ☆ ☆   *Ease of Reading :* ① ② ③ ④ ⑤

WHO WILL I RECOMMEND IT TO?

WHY I READ IT?

FAVORITE QUOTE : "

WHAT IT INSPIRED ME TO?
(read/learn/visit)

"

Book Tracker

BOOK TITLE	AUTHOR	PAGE	DONE

76

BOOK TITLE :

AUTHOR :   **PAGES :**

PUBLISHER :   **PUB DATE :**

○ PAPERBACK   ○ HARDBACK   ○ E-BOOK   ○ AUDIOBOOK   ○ FICTION   ○ NON-FICTION

SOURCE :   ○ BOUGHT   ○ LOANED   **FROM :**

Genre :

Start Date :   *Finished Date :*

MY THOUGHTS :   *Rating :* ☆ ☆ ☆ ☆ ☆   *Ease of Reading :* ① ② ③ ④ ⑤

FAVORITE QUOTE : "

WHO WILL I RECOMMEND IT TO?

WHY I READ IT?

WHAT IT INSPIRED ME TO?
(read/learn/visit)

77

BOOK TITLE :

AUTHOR :   **PAGES :**

PUBLISHER :   **PUB DATE :**

○ PAPERBACK   ○ HARDBACK   ○ E-BOOK   ○ AUDIOBOOK   ○ FICTION   ○ NON-FICTION

SOURCE :   ○ BOUGHT   ○ LOANED   **FROM :**

Genre :

Start Date :   *Finished Date* :

MY THOUGHTS :   *Rating :* ☆ ☆ ☆ ☆ ☆   *Ease of Reading :* ① ② ③ ④ ⑤

WHO WILL I RECOMMEND IT TO?

WHY I READ IT?

FAVORITE QUOTE : "

WHAT IT INSPIRED ME TO?
(read/learn/visit)

"

78 BOOK TITLE : _____

AUTHOR : _____ PAGES : _____

PUBLISHER : _____ PUB DATE : _____

○ PAPERBACK   ○ HARDBACK   ○ E-BOOK   ○ AUDIOBOOK   ○ FICTION   ○ NON-FICTION

SOURCE : ○ BOUGHT   ○ LOANED   FROM : _____

Genre : _____

Start Date : _____   *Finished Date* : _____

MY THOUGHTS :   *Rating* : ☆ ☆ ☆ ☆ ☆   *Ease of Reading* : ① ② ③ ④ ⑤

_____
_____
_____
_____
_____
_____
_____
_____
_____
_____
_____
_____
_____
_____

WHO WILL I RECOMMEND IT TO?

WHY I READ IT?

FAVORITE QUOTE : "

WHAT IT INSPIRED ME TO?
(read/learn/visit)

"

79

BOOK TITLE :

AUTHOR :   **PAGES :**

PUBLISHER :   **PUB DATE :**

○ PAPERBACK   ○ HARDBACK   ○ E-BOOK   ○ AUDIOBOOK   ○ FICTION   ○ NON-FICTION

SOURCE :   ○ BOUGHT   ○ LOANED   **FROM :**

Genre :

Start Date :   *Finished Date :*

MY THOUGHTS :   *Rating :* ☆ ☆ ☆ ☆ ☆   *Ease of Reading :* ① ② ③ ④ ⑤

WHO WILL I RECOMMEND IT TO?

WHY I READ IT?

FAVORITE QUOTE : "

WHAT IT INSPIRED ME TO?
(read/learn/visit)

"

80 BOOK TITLE :

AUTHOR :   **PAGES :**

PUBLISHER :   **PUB DATE :**

○ PAPERBACK ○ HARDBACK ○ E-BOOK ○ AUDIOBOOK   ○ FICTION ○ NON-FICTION

SOURCE : ○ BOUGHT   ○ LOANED   **FROM :**

Genre :

Start Date :   *Finished Date* :

MY THOUGHTS :   *Rating* : ☆ ☆ ☆ ☆ ☆   *Ease of Reading* : ① ② ③ ④ ⑤

WHO WILL I RECOMMEND IT TO?

WHY I READ IT?

FAVORITE QUOTE : "

WHAT IT INSPIRED ME TO?
(read/learn/visit)

"

81

BOOK TITLE :

AUTHOR :   **PAGES :**

PUBLISHER :   **PUB DATE :**

○ PAPERBACK   ○ HARDBACK   ○ E-BOOK   ○ AUDIOBOOK   ○ FICTION   ○ NON-FICTION

SOURCE :   ○ BOUGHT   ○ LOANED   **FROM :**

Genre :

Start Date :   *Finished Date :*

MY THOUGHTS :   *Rating :* ☆ ☆ ☆ ☆ ☆   *Ease of Reading :* ① ② ③ ④ ⑤

WHO WILL I RECOMMEND IT TO?

WHY I READ IT?

FAVORITE QUOTE : "

WHAT IT INSPIRED ME TO?
(read/learn/visit)

"

82 BOOK TITLE :

AUTHOR :   PAGES :

PUBLISHER :   PUB DATE :

○ PAPERBACK   ○ HARDBACK   ○ E-BOOK   ○ AUDIOBOOK   ○ FICTION   ○ NON-FICTION

SOURCE : ○ BOUGHT   ○ LOANED   FROM :

Genre :

Start Date :   Finished Date :

MY THOUGHTS :   Rating : ☆ ☆ ☆ ☆ ☆   Ease of Reading : ① ② ③ ④ ⑤

WHO WILL I RECOMMEND IT TO?

WHY I READ IT?

FAVORITE QUOTE : "

WHAT IT INSPIRED ME TO?
(read/learn/visit)

83

BOOK TITLE :

AUTHOR :   **PAGES :**

PUBLISHER :   **PUB DATE :**

○ PAPERBACK   ○ HARDBACK   ○ E-BOOK   ○ AUDIOBOOK   ○ FICTION   ○ NON-FICTION

SOURCE :   ○ BOUGHT   ○ LOANED   FROM :

Genre :

Start Date :   *Finished Date* :

MY THOUGHTS :   *Rating* : ☆ ☆ ☆ ☆ ☆   *Ease of Reading* : ① ② ③ ④ ⑤

WHO WILL I RECOMMEND IT TO?

WHY I READ IT?

FAVORITE QUOTE : "

WHAT IT INSPIRED ME TO?
(read/learn/visit)

"

84 BOOK TITLE :

AUTHOR :   **PAGES :**

PUBLISHER :   **PUB DATE :**

○ PAPERBACK   ○ HARDBACK   ○ E-BOOK   ○ AUDIOBOOK   ○ FICTION   ○ NON-FICTION

SOURCE : ○ BOUGHT   ○ LOANED   **FROM :**

Genre :

Start Date :   *Finished Date* :

MY THOUGHTS :   *Rating :* ☆ ☆ ☆ ☆ ☆   *Ease of Reading :* ① ② ③ ④ ⑤

FAVORITE QUOTE : "

WHO WILL I RECOMMEND IT TO?

WHY I READ IT?

WHAT IT INSPIRED ME TO?
(read/learn/visit)

"

85

BOOK TITLE :

AUTHOR :   **PAGES :**

PUBLISHER :   **PUB DATE :**

○ PAPERBACK   ○ HARDBACK   ○ E-BOOK   ○ AUDIOBOOK   ○ FICTION   ○ NON-FICTION

SOURCE :   ○ BOUGHT   ○ LOANED   FROM :

Genre :

Start Date :   *Finished Date* :

MY THOUGHTS :   *Rating* : ☆ ☆ ☆ ☆ ☆   *Ease of Reading* : ① ② ③ ④ ⑤

WHO WILL I RECOMMEND IT TO?

WHY I READ IT?

FAVORITE QUOTE : "

WHAT IT INSPIRED ME TO?
(read/learn/visit)

"

86

BOOK TITLE :

AUTHOR :   **PAGES :**

PUBLISHER :   **PUB DATE :**

○ PAPERBACK   ○ HARDBACK   ○ E-BOOK   ○ AUDIOBOOK   ○ FICTION   ○ NON-FICTION

SOURCE : ○ BOUGHT   ○ LOANED   FROM :

Genre :

Start Date :   *Finished Date :*

MY THOUGHTS :   *Rating :* ☆ ☆ ☆ ☆ ☆   *Ease of Reading :* ① ② ③ ④ ⑤

WHO WILL I RECOMMEND IT TO?

WHY I READ IT?

FAVORITE QUOTE : "

WHAT IT INSPIRED ME TO?
(read/learn/visit)

"

87

BOOK TITLE :

AUTHOR :   **PAGES :**

PUBLISHER :   **PUB DATE :**

○ PAPERBACK   ○ HARDBACK   ○ E-BOOK   ○ AUDIOBOOK   ○ FICTION   ○ NON-FICTION

SOURCE :   ○ BOUGHT   ○ LOANED   FROM :

Genre :

Start Date :   *Finished Date* :

MY THOUGHTS :   *Rating* : ☆ ☆ ☆ ☆ ☆   *Ease of Reading* : ① ② ③ ④ ⑤

WHO WILL I RECOMMEND IT TO?

WHY I READ IT?

FAVORITE QUOTE : "

WHAT IT INSPIRED ME TO?
(read/learn/visit)

"

88 BOOK TITLE :

AUTHOR :   PAGES :

PUBLISHER :   **PUB DATE :**

○ PAPERBACK   ○ HARDBACK   ○ E-BOOK   ○ AUDIOBOOK   ○ FICTION   ○ NON-FICTION

SOURCE :   ○ BOUGHT   ○ LOANED   **FROM :**

Genre :

Start Date :   *Finished Date* :

MY THOUGHTS :   *Rating* : ☆ ☆ ☆ ☆ ☆   *Ease of Reading* : ① ② ③ ④ ⑤

FAVORITE QUOTE : "

WHO WILL I RECOMMEND IT TO?

WHY I READ IT?

WHAT IT INSPIRED ME TO?
(read/learn/visit)

"

89 BOOK TITLE :

AUTHOR : _____ PAGES : _____

PUBLISHER : _____ PUB DATE : _____

○ PAPERBACK   ○ HARDBACK   ○ E-BOOK   ○ AUDIOBOOK   ○ FICTION   ○ NON-FICTION

SOURCE : ○ BOUGHT   ○ LOANED   FROM : _____

Genre : _____

Start Date : _____   *Finished Date* : _____

MY THOUGHTS :   *Rating* : ☆ ☆ ☆ ☆ ☆   *Ease of Reading* : ① ② ③ ④ ⑤

WHO WILL I RECOMMEND IT TO?

WHY I READ IT?

FAVORITE QUOTE : "

WHAT IT INSPIRED ME TO?
(read/learn/visit)

"

90 BOOK TITLE :

AUTHOR :   PAGES :

PUBLISHER :   **PUB DATE :**

○ PAPERBACK   ○ HARDBACK   ○ E-BOOK   ○ AUDIOBOOK   ○ FICTION   ○ NON-FICTION

SOURCE :   ○ BOUGHT   ○ LOANED   FROM :

Genre :

Start Date :   *Finished Date* :

MY THOUGHTS :   *Rating* : ☆ ☆ ☆ ☆ ☆   *Ease of Reading* : ① ② ③ ④ ⑤

WHO WILL I RECOMMEND IT TO?

WHY I READ IT?

FAVORITE QUOTE : "

WHAT IT INSPIRED ME TO?
(read/learn/visit)

"

91

BOOK TITLE :

AUTHOR :   **PAGES :**

PUBLISHER :   **PUB DATE :**

○ PAPERBACK   ○ HARDBACK   ○ E-BOOK   ○ AUDIOBOOK   ○ FICTION   ○ NON-FICTION

SOURCE :   ○ BOUGHT   ○ LOANED   **FROM :**

Genre :

Start Date :   *Finished Date :*

MY THOUGHTS :   *Rating :* ☆ ☆ ☆ ☆ ☆   *Ease of Reading :* ① ② ③ ④ ⑤

WHO WILL I RECOMMEND IT TO?

WHY I READ IT?

FAVORITE QUOTE : "

WHAT IT INSPIRED ME TO?
(read/learn/visit)

"

92

BOOK TITLE :

AUTHOR :   **PAGES :**

PUBLISHER :   **PUB DATE :**

○ PAPERBACK   ○ HARDBACK   ○ E-BOOK   ○ AUDIOBOOK   ○ FICTION   ○ NON-FICTION

SOURCE : ○ BOUGHT   ○ LOANED   **FROM :**

Genre :

Start Date :   *Finished Date* :

MY THOUGHTS :   *Rating* : ☆ ☆ ☆ ☆ ☆   *Ease of Reading* : ① ② ③ ④ ⑤

FAVORITE QUOTE : "

WHO WILL I RECOMMEND IT TO?

WHY I READ IT?

WHAT IT INSPIRED ME TO?
(read/learn/visit)

"

93

BOOK TITLE :

AUTHOR :   **PAGES :**

PUBLISHER :   **PUB DATE :**

○ PAPERBACK ○ HARDBACK ○ E-BOOK ○ AUDIOBOOK   ○ FICTION ○ NON-FICTION

SOURCE : ○ BOUGHT   ○ LOANED   **FROM :**

Genre :

Start Date :   *Finished Date* :

MY THOUGHTS :   *Rating :* ☆ ☆ ☆ ☆ ☆   *Ease of Reading :* ① ② ③ ④ ⑤

WHO WILL I RECOMMEND IT TO?

WHY I READ IT?

FAVORITE QUOTE : "

WHAT IT INSPIRED ME TO?
(read/learn/visit)

"

94 BOOK TITLE :

AUTHOR :   PAGES :

PUBLISHER :   PUB DATE :

○ PAPERBACK   ○ HARDBACK   ○ E-BOOK   ○ AUDIOBOOK   ○ FICTION   ○ NON-FICTION

SOURCE :   ○ BOUGHT   ○ LOANED   FROM :

Genre :

Start Date :   *Finished Date* :

MY THOUGHTS :   *Rating* : ☆ ☆ ☆ ☆ ☆   *Ease of Reading* : ① ② ③ ④ ⑤

FAVORITE QUOTE : "

WHO WILL I RECOMMEND IT TO?

WHY I READ IT?

WHAT IT INSPIRED ME TO?
(read/learn/visit)

95

BOOK TITLE :

AUTHOR :   **PAGES :**

PUBLISHER :   **PUB DATE :**

○ PAPERBACK   ○ HARDBACK   ○ E-BOOK   ○ AUDIOBOOK   ○ FICTION   ○ NON-FICTION

SOURCE :   ○ BOUGHT   ○ LOANED   FROM :

Genre :

Start Date :   *Finished Date* :

MY THOUGHTS :   *Rating* : ☆ ☆ ☆ ☆ ☆   *Ease of Reading* : ① ② ③ ④ ⑤

WHO WILL I RECOMMEND IT TO?

WHY I READ IT?

FAVORITE QUOTE : "

WHAT IT INSPIRED ME TO?
(read/learn/visit)

"

96

BOOK TITLE : _____

AUTHOR : _____ **PAGES :** _____

PUBLISHER : _____ **PUB DATE :** _____

○ PAPERBACK ○ HARDBACK ○ E-BOOK ○ AUDIOBOOK ○ FICTION ○ NON-FICTION

SOURCE : ○ BOUGHT ○ LOANED **FROM :** _____

Genre : _____

Start Date : _____ _Finished Date_ : _____

MY THOUGHTS : _Rating_ : ☆ ☆ ☆ ☆ ☆ _Ease of Reading_ : ① ② ③ ④ ⑤

_____

_____

_____

_____

_____

_____

_____

_____

_____

_____

_____

_____

_____

_____

WHO WILL I RECOMMEND IT TO?

WHY I READ IT?

FAVORITE QUOTE : "

WHAT IT INSPIRED ME TO?
(read/learn/visit)

"

97 BOOK TITLE :

AUTHOR :   PAGES :

PUBLISHER :   PUB DATE :

○ PAPERBACK   ○ HARDBACK   ○ E-BOOK   ○ AUDIOBOOK   ○ FICTION   ○ NON-FICTION
SOURCE :   ○ BOUGHT   ○ LOANED   FROM :

Genre :

Start Date :   Finished Date :

MY THOUGHTS :   Rating : ☆ ☆ ☆ ☆ ☆   Ease of Reading : ① ② ③ ④ ⑤

WHO WILL I RECOMMEND IT TO?

WHY I READ IT?

FAVORITE QUOTE : "

WHAT IT INSPIRED ME TO?
(read/learn/visit)

"

98 BOOK TITLE :

AUTHOR :   PAGES :

PUBLISHER :   PUB DATE :

○ PAPERBACK   ○ HARDBACK   ○ E-BOOK   ○ AUDIOBOOK   ○ FICTION   ○ NON-FICTION

SOURCE :   ○ BOUGHT   ○ LOANED   FROM :

Genre :

Start Date :   Finished Date :

MY THOUGHTS :   Rating : ☆ ☆ ☆ ☆ ☆   Ease of Reading : ① ② ③ ④ ⑤

WHO WILL I RECOMMEND IT TO?

WHY I READ IT?

FAVORITE QUOTE : "

WHAT IT INSPIRED ME TO?
(read/learn/visit)

99 BOOK TITLE :

AUTHOR :   PAGES :

PUBLISHER :   PUB DATE :

○ PAPERBACK   ○ HARDBACK   ○ E-BOOK   ○ AUDIOBOOK   ○ FICTION   ○ NON-FICTION

SOURCE :   ○ BOUGHT   ○ LOANED   FROM :

Genre :

Start Date :   *Finished Date* :

MY THOUGHTS :   *Rating* : ☆ ☆ ☆ ☆ ☆   *Ease of Reading* : ① ② ③ ④ ⑤

WHO WILL I RECOMMEND IT TO?

WHY I READ IT?

FAVORITE QUOTE : "

WHAT IT INSPIRED ME TO?
(*read/learn/visit*)

"

100

BOOK TITLE :

AUTHOR :   **PAGES :**

PUBLISHER :   **PUB DATE :**

○ PAPERBACK   ○ HARDBACK   ○ E-BOOK   ○ AUDIOBOOK   ○ FICTION   ○ NON-FICTION

SOURCE :   ○ BOUGHT   ○ LOANED   **FROM :**

Genre :

Start Date :   *Finished Date :*

MY THOUGHTS :   *Rating :* ☆ ☆ ☆ ☆ ☆   *Ease of Reading :* ① ② ③ ④ ⑤

FAVORITE QUOTE : "

WHO WILL I RECOMMEND IT TO?

WHY I READ IT?

WHAT IT INSPIRED ME TO?
(read/learn/visit)

"

Book Tracker

BOOK TITLE	AUTHOR	PAGE	DONE

Wish list

TITLE	AUTHOR	PRICE	BOUGHT

Notes

Notes

Printed in Great Britain
by Amazon

13378995R00072